Let's Visit South Africa

Written by
Cath Jones

South Africa is a fantastic place to visit. There is so much to see and do.

When you arrive, you will need to get some money. South Africa uses money called the **rand**. There are one hundred **cents** in a rand.

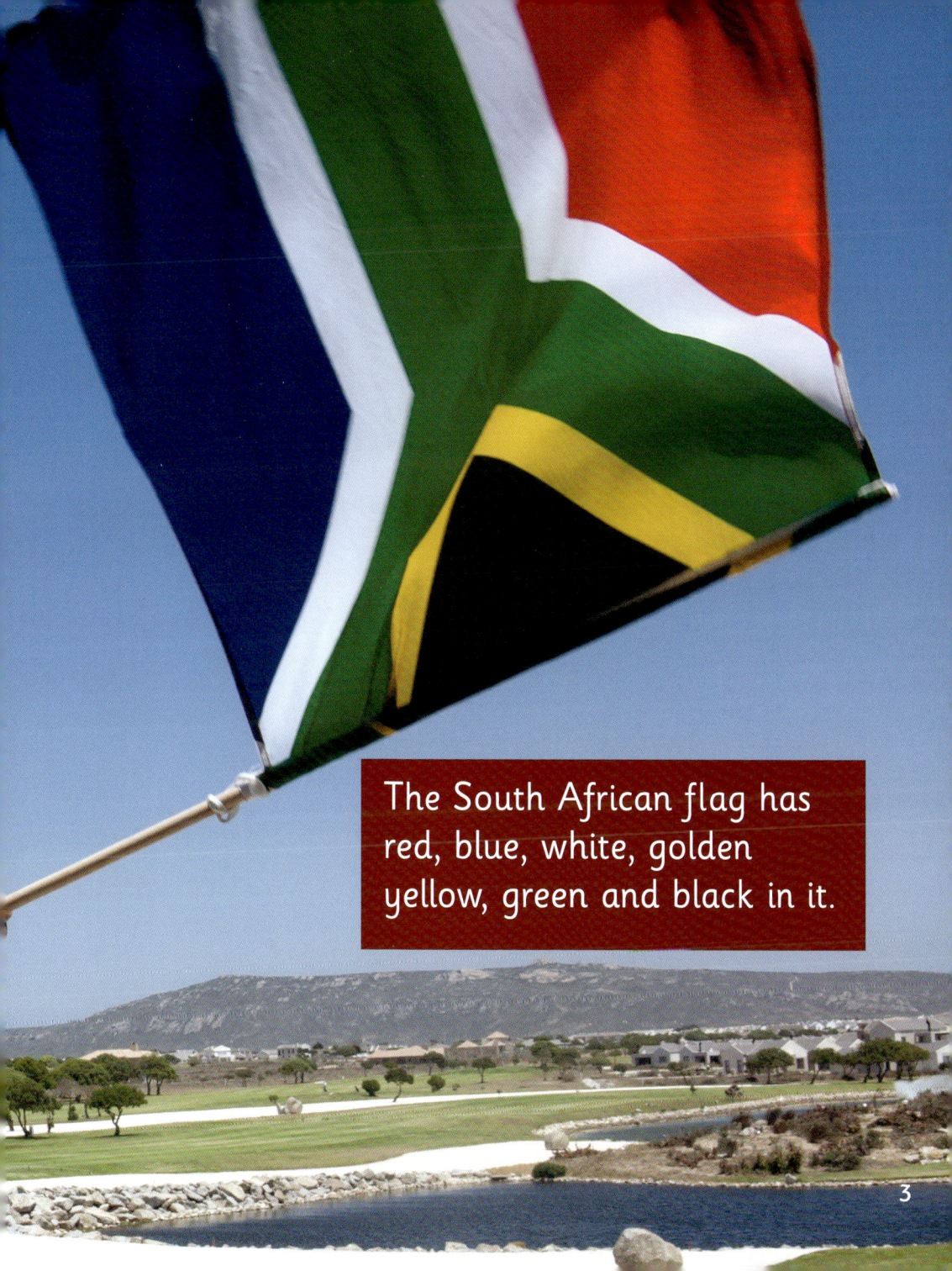

The South African flag has red, blue, white, golden yellow, green and black in it.

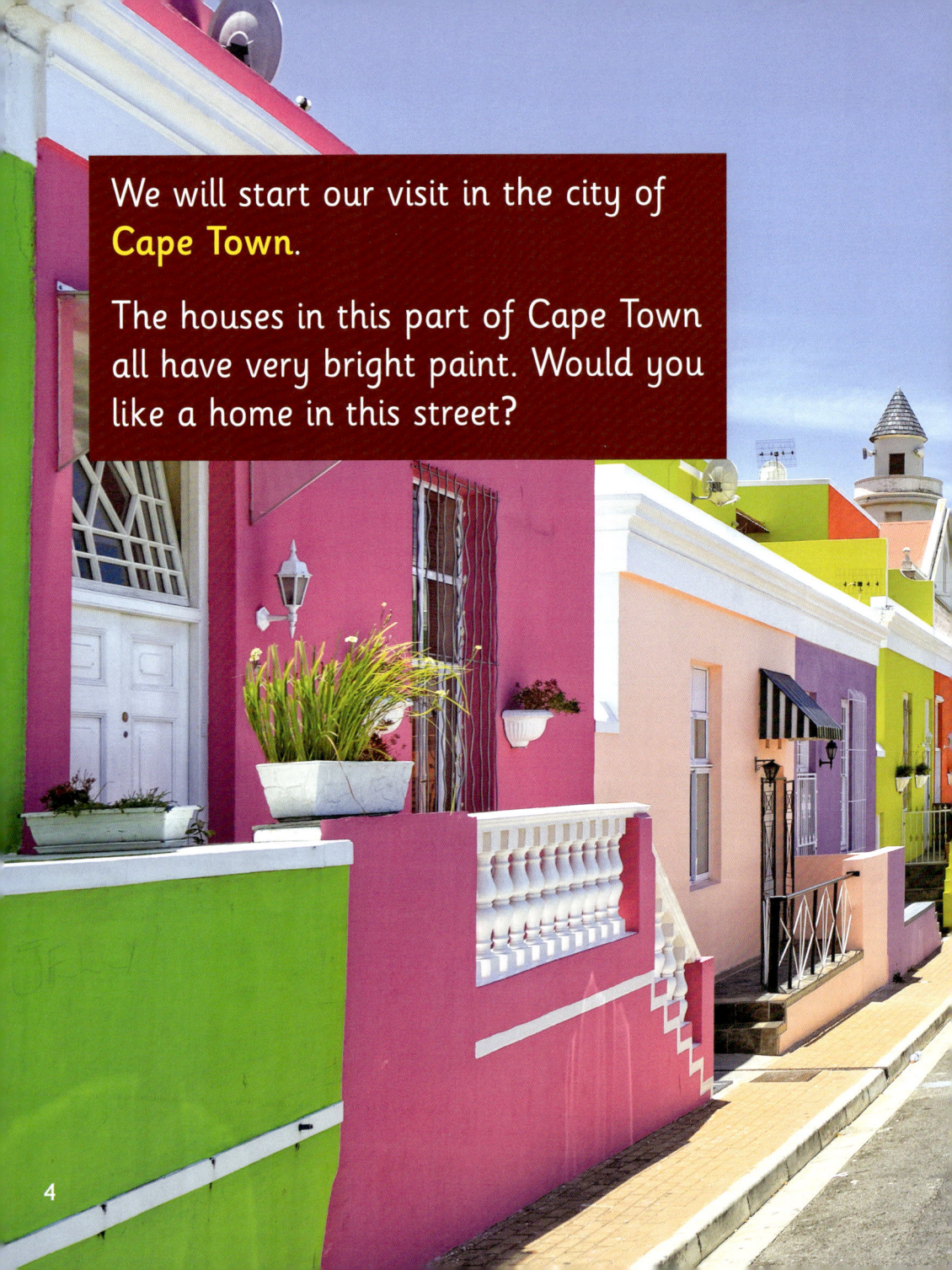

We will start our visit in the city of **Cape Town**.

The houses in this part of Cape Town all have very bright paint. Would you like a home in this street?

Every year there is a carnival in Cape Town. The children dress up and paint their faces.

Near Cape Town you will find good surfing, bright beach huts and miles and miles of sandy beaches.

But the sand might not all be for you, because look who has their home here on this rocky beach.

Now it's time to jump in a jeep.

I hope you have a camera with you, because the driver knows where you can see lots of animals.

This lion is quite sleepy. Will he sleep here on the grass?

Hush! Don't make any noise!

We don't want to spook the animals at the watering hole.

Look, they are wildebeest!

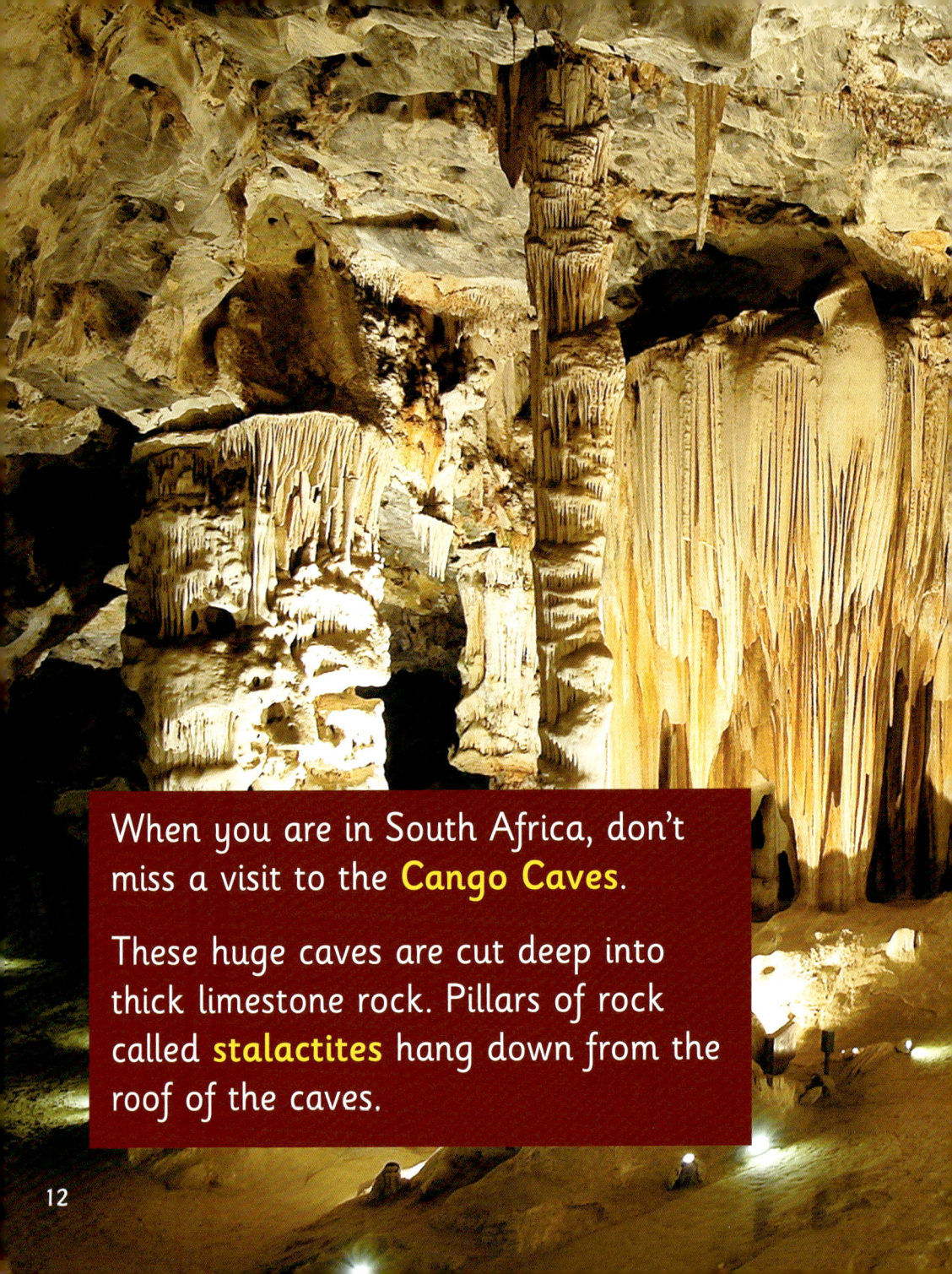

When you are in South Africa, don't miss a visit to the **Cango Caves**.

These huge caves are cut deep into thick limestone rock. Pillars of rock called **stalactites** hang down from the roof of the caves.

You can see cave paintings here too. People think they are tens of thousands of years old!

If you like trekking, South Africa has some fantastic nature trails.

You can even trek up a mountain to see the city of Cape Town from up high. That's quite a climb!

But watch out! Don't slip! That's a sheer drop.

We could take the pass down into **Hex River Valley** too.

Can you see the snow on the mountains?

Let's finish our trip with some shopping. You can spend plenty of money in modern shopping complexes or in open air markets.

But don't spend too much, because we need to fit everything into a travel bag!